Reading with Ricky
Frogs, Spiders, and Birds

Stories by Kathy Kranking
Illustrations by Christian Slade

Contents

2   **Quack! Quack!**

10   **Learn More: Frog Babies**

12   **The Game**

21   **Learn More: Spider Webs**

22   **The Show**

29   **Learn More: Winter Birds**

Quack! Quack!

Ricky Raccoon lay in bed with his pillow over his head. He had been trying to sleep for hours. But a strange noise was keeping him awake.

Quack! Quack-Quack! Quack! went the noise.

"Ugh!" said Ricky, sitting up. "How can I sleep with all that quacking? And what kind of ducks quack at night, anyway?"

Ricky got up and went to his window. The woods seemed to echo with the quacking sound. He sighed and went back to bed.

The next morning, after barely sleeping, Ricky groggily answered a knock at his door. It was Bizzie Beaver, grinning a wide-awake grin.

FLORA WONDERS

What do you think is keeping Ricky awake?

"Good morning, Ricky!" Bizzie said. Then he frowned. "Are you OK? You look really tired."

"I am," Ricky grumbled. "I was up almost all night because of that quacking. Didn't you hear it?"

"Nothing wakes me," said Bizzie. "Wait, did you say 'quacking'?"

"Yes," said Ricky. Then he noticed something. "Listen," he said. "I still hear it."

Ricky and Bizzie both listened, and sure enough they heard a quacking sound.

"They're still at it!" Ricky said. "Come on, let's go see who it is."

Ricky and Bizzie followed the sound. Ricky was still feeling sleepy, and he hadn't noticed that they were now at the edge of a pond. As Ricky yawned, his foot slipped, and he lost his balance.

Splash! Ricky landed in the cold water!

"Ricky!" Bizzie cried. "Are you OK?"

"Glub!" Ricky answered, spitting out a mouthful of water.

"Hey, what's that jelly all over you?" Bizzie asked.

Ricky looked down and saw that his fur was covered with clear, jelly-like stuff. "I don't know," he said. He rinsed the jelly off in the water, then climbed out of the pond.

"I don't hear the ducks anymore," Ricky said.

"What ducks?" asked a voice above them. Ricky and Bizzie looked up to see their friend Mrs. Cardinal sitting on a branch.

"Hi, Mrs. C!" they called.

"A bunch of ducks were quacking all night long," Ricky explained. "And then when we looked for them, I fell into this pond and got covered with some sort of weird goo."

Mrs. C smiled. "I can explain both of those things with a single word," she said. "Frogs!"

Ricky and Bizzie looked at each other. "Huh?" they asked.

"At this time of year," Mrs. C explained, "a kind of frog called a wood frog calls for mates. The frogs' calls sound like ducks quacking. And that gooey stuff you fell into is actually the frogs' jelly-like eggs!"

"Frog eggs!" said Ricky. "Wow, I'm glad I put them back into the water."

"You should come to the pond in a few weeks," said Mrs. C. "The eggs will probably have hatched by then."

So a few weeks later, Ricky and Bizzie did go back. And they brought Flora Skunk and Mitzi Mink with them.

"I can't wait to see the cute baby frogs!" Flora said excitedly as they walked to the pond.

When they got there, the four friends lay on their bellies to see the babies. But to their surprise, they didn't see any tiny frogs.

BIZZIE WANTS TO KNOW

How are frog eggs different from chicken eggs?

"I don't see anything except some little brown fish," said Mitzi.

"Those aren't fish. They're tadpoles," said a familiar voice. It was Mrs.C.

"Tadpoles are frog babies," she explained. "As they get bigger, they lose their tails, grow legs, and turn into frogs! Then they leave the water. But they'll be back next year to lay eggs."

Ricky studied the tiny tadpoles. "Well, I guess that means I'll be seeing you—I mean, hearing you—then!" he said.

RICKY ASKS

Why didn't we see any baby frogs?

LEARN MORE

Frog Babies

Frog babies go through big changes as they grow up.

1 A female frog lays soft, jelly-covered eggs in the water.

2 Tadpoles hatch from the eggs.

3 Before long, a tadpole grows back legs and then front legs.

4 The tadpole's tail starts to shrink. The tadpole has now become a froglet.

5 The froglet becomes a frog when its tail is gone. It is ready to live part of its life on land.

Game Day

It was a crisp fall afternoon. The leaves were turning pretty shades of yellow, red, and orange.

"What should we do today?" Ricky Raccoon asked his friends. He was sitting with Flora Skunk, Bizzie Beaver, and Flora's little brother, Sammy Skunk.

"I know," said Flora. "Let's play football!"

"Great idea!" said Ricky and Bizzie.

"But I don't know how to play football," said Sammy.

"Don't worry, we'll teach you," said Ricky. "I'll get my football and meet you at Sunny Meadow."

A little while later, the friends had gathered to play. "OK, Sammy," Flora said. "Go over by that tree, and we'll pass the ball to you."

Sammy ran toward the tree, then turned around and waited.

Flora stood over the ball and bent down. Ricky lined up behind Flora and called, "Hike! Hike!" Flora hiked the ball, and Ricky turned and threw it toward Sammy.

But Sammy was confused, so he started to walk back toward his friends. "You want to take a hike?" he asked. "I thought we were playing footba—ugh!" The ball hit Sammy in the chest and bounced to the ground.

RICKY WONDERS

Why didn't Sammy try to catch the ball?

BOUNCE!

"I'm sorry, Sammy!" said Ricky. "Why didn't you try to catch the ball?"

"Because you said 'hike,'" said Sammy.

"That's football talk," Bizzie explained. "It means he wants Flora to give him the football so he can throw it."

"Oh," Sammy said.

"Let's try again," said Flora.

Sammy went out for another pass. As he jumped up to catch the ball, it hit his paw, and he missed it. "Rats!" he said.

"Don't worry, Sammy," said Ricky. "You'll get the next one."

Ricky threw a nice high pass. Keeping his eyes glued to the ball, Sammy reached up as the ball was almost to him. He was just about to catch it when he ran face-first into something sticky.

FLORA WANTS TO KNOW

What did Sammy run into?

"Aaargh!" Sammy yelled, pulling up short as the ball sailed past him. He pawed at his face.

"Help!" he shouted, as the others came running up.

"What happened?" asked Flora.

"There's something yucky all over me!" the little skunk said.

"Oh," said Ricky, pulling at a sticky strand on Sammy's ear. "It looks like you ran into a spider web!"

"Ew!" Sammy cried. "There's not a spider on me, is there?"

"No, you're fine," said Flora, as she helped wipe the spider web from Sammy's face.

"I don't want to play anymore," whined Sammy.

"Come on," said Flora. "We'll go home and get you cleaned up. Sorry, guys," she said to Ricky and Bizzie.

"It's OK," Ricky said. "Let's meet tomorrow and try again."

The next day, Ricky and Bizzie were tossing the football back and forth as Flora and Sammy came up.

"Hi, guys!" said Bizzie. "Ready to play?"

"Nah," said Sammy. "I'm no good. I'll just watch."

"Aw, come on, Sammy," said Ricky. "Don't give up."

But Sammy had already wandered away and didn't seem to be listening. Suddenly he said, "Hey, guys! Come over here."

The others walked over and Sammy pointed. "This is where I ran into the spider web yesterday. Look!"

The others gasped. There, between the bushes, was a brand new spider web, right where the old one had been. And sitting in it was the spider!

"Wow!" said Flora. "That spider made a new web last night!"

"Look how pretty it is," said Ricky. "Spiders are really talented!"

"They sure are," said Sammy. "I like the spider web—now that I'm not in it!" He thought for a second. Then he said, "Come on, let's play football!"

"I thought you didn't want to play," said Flora. "What changed your mind?"

"Well," said Sammy, "that spider didn't give up. So I won't either!"

BIZZIE ASKS

Can you think of a time when you didn't give up?

Spider Webs

Different kinds of spiders make different-shaped webs.

Orb-weaver spiders make round webs.

Sheet-web spiders make flat webs.

Funnel-web spiders make webs that are shaped like funnels.

The Show

It was a crisp winter morning. Flora Skunk stopped in surprise as she headed out her front door. Someone had slipped a sign under the door. It said, "Come see the show!"

"What show?" said Flora to herself.

At around the same time, Bizzie Beaver was coming out of his lodge. As he did, he saw a piece of paper was poked onto one of the sticks. The paper said, "Big show today! Don't miss it!"

Not far away, Mitzi Mink noticed a sign on a nearby tree. The sign said, "Show today! Come one! Come all!"

"I wonder what this means," said Mitzi, pulling the sign off the tree. As she continued down the path, she saw Flora walking toward her. She was holding the sign that had been under her door. Soon, Bizzie Beaver came along. He was holding the sign that had been on his lodge.

"So you got one, too!" said Flora.

"I found this one hanging on a tree!" Mitzi said.

"What kind of show do you think it is?" Bizzie asked.

BIZZIE WONDERS

What do you think the show will be about?

"Let's find Ricky," said Flora. "Maybe he knows something about this show."

When the friends got to Ricky Raccoon's home, he was outside.

"Hey, Ricky," said Mitzi. "Do you know anything about a show that's supposed to happen?"

Ricky smiled mysteriously. "Maybe," he said. "But first, will you help me with some things?"

"Sure," they said, as Ricky led them over to the picnic table. On it were pine cones, a jar of peanut butter, spoons, and string.

"First, we're going to spread this peanut butter onto the pine cones," Ricky explained.

The others looked at each other. Then they looked back at Ricky. "Are you on some kind of new diet?" asked Mitzi.

But Ricky just smiled. He scooped out a big spoonful of peanut butter and smeared it all over a pine cone.

Bizzie, Flora, and Mitzi each picked up a pine cone. They spread the peanut butter onto the cones as Ricky had. They kept going until all the cones were covered.

FLORA WANTS TO KNOW

What are we going to do with the pine cones?

"Now," said Ricky, "we'll tie the strings to the pine cones."
As they began tying, Mitzi said, "So, about that show...."

Ricky smiled. "You'll see," he said. Then Ricky went inside his house. A few minutes later he came back carrying something.

"A bird feeder!" said Flora.

"Yup," said Ricky. "Can you help me hang it from this branch?" Everyone worked together to hang the bird feeder. Then the four friends hung the pine cones.

"Now let's sit down," said Ricky. "It's show time!"

"What do you mean?" asked Bizzie.

"Wait and see," Ricky said.

The friends waited. Soon they heard a soft flapping sound, as a bird flew past them and landed on the feeder.

"Look!" whispered Flora.

The bird cocked its head and peeked around. Then it began eating the birdseed.

Soon another bird landed on the feeder. Then a bird flew down onto one of the pine cones and began eating the peanut butter.

More and more birds kept coming, until all kinds of birds were fluttering back and forth around the feeders.

"See?" said Ricky with a big grin. "Welcome to the show!"

Winter Bir-r-rds

Find out what some birds do during
the winter with these read-aloud poems.

Poems by Jennifer Bové

Blue Jay

Brrr, it is chilly
In a winter storm.
But fluffing up her feathers
Helps Blue Jay stay warm.

Pick-peck, Chickadee checks
For goodies she can munch.
The seeds inside these spruce cones
Make the perfect winter lunch.

Chickadee

Cardinal needs a break
From the wind and snow.
The shelter of a tree
Is a cozy place to go.

Cardinal

Published by the National Wildlife Federation.

"Ricky and Pals" originally appeared in RANGER RICK JR, a publication for children ages 4–7 in the Ranger Rick family of magazines.

Kathy Kranking, Author
Christian Slade, Illustrator
Molly Woods, Reading Consultant

Photo and Illustration Credits:
Page 10: David Tipling / Biosphoto; Page 11: David Cheshire / Alamy Stock Photo (top left), Dave Pressland / FLPA / Minden Pictures (top right), Jef Meul / NIS / Minden Pictures (bottom left), pqpictures.co.uk / Alamy Stock Photos (bottom right); Page 21: Alexander Vidal; Page 29: Jerry Acton; Page 30: Alan Murphy; Page 31: Woodfall / Avalon.red.

Printed in the United States of America.

RangerRick.org

ISBN: 978-1-947254-25-1